Kathy —

Now that school's over there might be a few quiet moments for a book of your choice!

We love you and are so proud of your accomplishment.

God bless you.

Love,
Rick and Caron

May 1981

His Name Is
WONDERFUL

HIS NAME IS
WONDERFUL
by Warren W. Wiersbe

**Tyndale House
Publishers, Inc.
Wheaton, Illinois**

Coverdale House
Publishers, Ltd.
Eastbourne, England

Cover photo by Robert McKendrick
Inside photos by Karl Fliehler & Gary Irving

Library of Congress
Catalog Card Number 76-42116
ISBN 0-8423-1435-0, cloth;
0-8423-1436-9, paper
Copyright © 1976
Tyndale House Publishers, Inc.,
Wheaton, Illinois.
All rights reserved.
First printing,
October 1976.
Printed in the
United States of America.

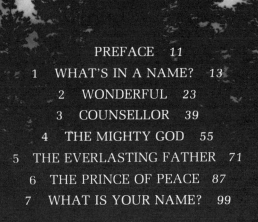

PREFACE

During twenty-five years of ministry, I have operated on the conviction that Jesus Christ is all that we need, that he is totally sufficient for whatever life brings to us.

That conviction is spelled out in this little book of essay-meditations. These chapters grew out of a series of Advent messages I gave at Moody Church in Chicago in 1975. Many of the people who heard them were kind enough to tell me they were helped by them, thus encouraging me to put them into this permanent form.

I pray that these meditations will help you, and that you will know for yourself how thrilling it is to have the government of your life on Christ's shoulder.

Warren Wiersbe
Moody Church, Chicago
April 1, 1976

ONE
What's in a Name?

Juliet asked Romeo that question and answered it herself: "What's in a name? That which we call a rose, by any other word would smell as sweet."

Granted, fair Juliet. But you and I and Romeo are *people*, not plants; and we know what our names are. Names make a difference to people. Why do people go to court to have their names changed? And why do parents agonize over the names they choose for their children? At some point in our childhood, many of us complained about our names and gave thanks when somebody pinned a nickname on us. In later years, no doubt, we dropped the nickname, but at least it took us through those dangerous years when the mention of a boy's name could be a declaration of war. One psychologist studied the names of 15,000 juvenile delinquents and discovered that those with odd or embarrassing names were in trouble four times as much as the others. Names do make a difference—if not to roses, at least to people.

Names are especially meaningful when you move into the world of the Bible. God named the first man "Adam," because he was made from the dust of the ground. "Adam" means "earth." God changed Abram's name to "Abraham" which means "the father of many nations," a perfect description of the patriarch. When God told the aged Abraham and Sarah they were going to have a son, they laughed, so their son was named "Isaac"—"laughter." That's a much happier choice than Rachel's when she named her boy "Ben-o-ni" which means "son of my sorrow." Of course, she was dying when she chose the name, but it was still a terrible weight to hang on any boy. Imagine going through life with a name that reminded you that your birth killed your mother! Jacob wisely changed the name to "Benjamin"—"son of my right hand." Jesus changed Simon's name to Peter—"a rock." At the time, the fisherman looked more like shifting sand, but Jesus saw the potential that was there and helped him to live up to his new name.

Yes, names make a difference in the world of the Bible, and the most important names are those associated with our Savior. "Thou shalt call his name Jesus: for he shall save his people from their sins" (Matthew 1:21).

"Jesus" is the Greek form of the Hebrew name "Joshua"; and both of them mean "the Lord is salvation." There are hundreds of names and titles of Jesus Christ in the Bible, and each one is a dual revelation to us. It reveals what Jesus Christ is in himself, and also what he wants to do for us. Each name that he bears indicates some blessing that he shares.

Seven hundred years before Jesus was born, the prophet Isaiah saw him coming. His record is in Isaiah 9:6: "For unto us a child is born, unto us a son is given: and the government shall be upon his shoulder: and his name shall be called Wonderful, Counsellor, The mighty God, The everlasting Father, The Prince of Peace." Isaiah saw that this child was unique; he was "born" and he was "given." In other words, this child was both God and man! As man, he was *born* and shared in sinless human nature. As God, he was *given*—the Father's love-gift to a sinful world. This child would be God in human flesh!

What would this child do? He would grow up and one day take the government of mankind upon his shoulder and bring order and peace to a world filled with confusion and war. But before taking the government upon his shoulder, he would first take a cross upon his shoulder, and then die upon that cross, bearing in his body the sins of the world. Before he could wear the diadem of glory as King of kings, he had to wear a shameful crown of thorns and give his life as a sacrifice for the sins of the world. The kingly Lion of the tribe of Judah first had to come as the lowly Lamb of God, for until sin had been paid for, God's righteous government could not be established.

There is but a little space between the words *given* and *and* in Isaiah 9:6, but they represent (so far) nineteen centuries of history. Jesus Christ finished his work on earth and returned to heaven, promising that he would come again. One day he shall return to this earth and take the government upon his shoulder. Isaiah saw that event, too.

"Of the increase of his government and peace there shall be no end, upon the throne of David, and upon his kingdom, to order it, and to establish it with judgment and with justice from henceforth even for ever. The zeal of the Lord of hosts will perform this." (9:7)

"But with righteousness shall he judge the poor.... The wolf also shall dwell with the lamb, and the leopard shall lie down with the kid; and the calf and the young lion and the fatling together; and a little child shall lead them.... They shall not hurt nor destroy in all my holy mountain: for the earth shall be full of the knowledge of the Lord, as the waters cover the sea." (11:4, 6, 9)

"Then the eyes of the blind shall be opened, and the ears of the deaf shall be unstopped. Then shall the lame man leap as an hart, and the tongue of the dumb sing: for in the wilderness shall waters break out, and streams in the desert.... And the ransomed of the Lord shall return, and come to Zion with songs and everlasting joy upon their heads: they shall obtain joy and gladness, and sorrow and sighing shall flee away." (35:5, 6, 10)

What a marvelous world it will be when Jesus Christ returns to take the government upon his shoulder!

But must we wait until then before we can enjoy his reign? No! *You and I can turn the government of our lives over to him today!* And when we do, all that is expressed in his names will become real in our own daily experience— Wonderful, Counsellor, The mighty God, The everlasting Father, The Prince of Peace.

His name is *Wonderful*: this takes care of the *dullness* of life. We no longer need to live on the cheap substitutes of the world in order to have excitement and enjoyment. Jesus Christ makes everything wonderful.

His name is *Counsellor*: this takes care of the *decisions* of life. We no longer will be baffled by the problems of life, wondering what step to take next. With Jesus Christ as our Counsellor, we will have the wisdom that we need to make the right decisions.

His name is *The mighty God*: this takes care of the *demands* of life. And life *is* demanding! Sometimes we feel like giving up; but through Jesus Christ, we can have the strength that we need to continue—and to conquer.

His name is *The everlasting Father:* this takes care of the *dimensions* of life. We can become a part of eternity! A whole new dimension of living can be ours through Jesus Christ, when the government of our life is on his shoulder.

His name is *The Prince of Peace:* this takes care of the *disturbances* of life. How we long for lasting peace within! What we would not give for the secret of poise and confidence in a threatening world! The answer is—Jesus Christ. He is The Prince of Peace, and when he controls the government of your life, he gives you peace.

It is not enough to trust Jesus Christ as Savior from sin, although that is certainly the beginning of his reign in our lives. We must also surrender our all to him and let him be the Lord of our lives. We must, by faith, place the government of our lives upon his shoulder. For you, individually, it means surrendering your *body* to him "a living sacrifice" (Romans 12:1), so that he can walk in your body and work through your body to accomplish his purposes on earth. It also means yielding your *mind* and learning his truth from his Word. "And be not conformed to this world: but be ye transformed by the renewing of your mind..." (Romans 12:2a). It also means giving him your *will*, "...that ye may prove what is that good, and

acceptable, and perfect, will of God"
(Romans 12:2b). Finally, it means giving
him your *heart*, your love. "If ye love
me, keep my commandments" (John
14:15). When he has your body, mind,
will, and heart, he can reign supreme in
your life. The government will be on
his shoulder, and all that he is will be
shared with you. You will experience
what it means to have him governing
your life as the One Who is Wonderful,
Counsellor, The mighty God, The
everlasting Father, and The Prince of
Peace.

Just now, by faith, put the
government of your life in his hands and
on his shoulder.

His name is
WONDERFUL
This takes care of the
dullness of life.
*Thou art the God that
doest wonders....*
PSALM 77:14

TWO

WONDERFUL

Bertrand Russell claimed that "at least half the sins of mankind" were caused by the fear of boredom. Perhaps this explains why children do not commit the kinds of sins that their elders commit, because, for the most part, children live in a world filled with wonder. A child can stare at a butterfly perched on a flower, or at fish swimming in a pool, and be perfectly content. Jesus may have had this in mind when he warned a group of adults, "Except ye be converted, and become as little children, ye shall not enter into the kingdom of heaven" (Matthew 18:3).

We are surrounded in this world by the miracles of modern science and yet people are bored, some of them to such an extent that they take their own lives. On the one hand we face a population explosion, and yet on the other hand millions of people are slowly dying of

the effects of loneliness and boredom.
Our cities are crowded and yet hearts are
empty. Henry Thoreau once defined the
city as "hundreds of people being lonely
together." In a world filled with all
sorts of electronic gadgets, you would
think that life would be exciting; but for
many people, life is just plain dull. They
look for new toys, and once the novelty
has worn off, they go back to the same
old routine. Obviously, something is
wrong.

Wonder vs. Novelty. What is
wonder? Many different concepts
cluster around this word: amazement,
surprise, astonishment, awe, admiration,
perhaps even bewilderment and
worship. The Hebrew word that Isaiah
used means "to separate, to distinguish."
Throughout the Old Testament, it is
translated a number of interesting
ways: marvelous, hidden, too high, too
difficult, miracle. It carries the basic
meaning of *being unique and different.*

But we must be careful to distinguish
wonder from some of the substitute ideas
that might lead us astray. True wonder
has *depth.* It is not a shallow emotion or
a passing wave of excitement. Wonder
penetrates; it goes much deeper than
sensationalism. The reason is that wonder
has *value;* it is not cheap amusement.
When a person experiences true
wonder, it enriches him and leaves him
a better person. Something wonderful
draws out of us the very best and puts
into us the very best. True wonder

creates in us an attitude of *humility:* we are overwhelmed and sense in ourselves the greatness of God and the littleness of man. David knew this feeling when he said, "When I consider thy heavens, the work of thy fingers, the moon and the stars, which thou hast ordained; what is man that thou art mindful of him? and the son of man, that thou visitest him?" (Psalm 8:3, 4).

Many people have the false notion that wonder is based on ignorance. Bring an ignorant savage to the big city and he will be amazed at the things that he sees! But true wonder is based on knowledge—the more we know, the more we wonder. The childlike spirit of wonder is not founded on innocent ignorance. It is founded upon an attitude of heart and mind toward reality. The wise man knows how little he really knows. Each trickle of truth only leads to the vast ocean of knowledge whose depths we cannot measure. Excitement over novelty passes when the novelty is explained and understood; but wonder grows deeper when knowledge increases. "To myself I seem to have been only like a boy playing on the seashore," wrote Sir Isaac Newton, "and diverting myself in now and then finding a smoother pebble or a prettier shell than ordinary, whilst the great ocean of truth lay all undiscovered before me." Albert Einstein put it this way: "The fairest thing we can experience is the mysterious.... He who knows it not, can no longer wonder, no longer feel amazement, is as good as dead, a snuffed out candle."

Finally, true wonder *possesses the whole person*, the mind and heart and will. Wonder is not an isolated experience that perplexes the mind only or merely stirs the emotions. True wonder captures the whole person; otherwise it is simply novelty or surprise. This is because true wonder is an attitude of life and not an interruption or an isolated event. The person who lives in childlike wonder always lives this way. Wonder is not something he turns on and off like a radio; it is the total outlook of his life at all times. In other words, all of him is involved in wonder all the time.

This kind of wonder is hard to find these days.

Substitutes for Wonder. Why is there so little true wonder in our world today? One reason is that the world is disappointing to most people. In every area of life we see nothing but problems: low wages and high prices, discrimination, political immorality, slums and smog and pollution, hypocrisy ... the list is a long one. The good suffer and the bad succeed. It is easy to develop a "what's-the-use" attitude, become cynical, pull into our own little world, and let the rest of the world go by.

But the real reason for our present-day loss of wonder goes much deeper. We are living in a mechanical world that is very impersonal. Most people look at the world and think of scientific law instead of a gracious Law-giver. We are persons, made in the image of God; therefore, we must have a personal world if life is to have any meaning. When life loses its meaning, life loses its wonder. We then become machines! A false view of science and technology has robbed us of a heavenly Father who makes the lilies more glorious than Solomon and who puts out his hand when the sparrow falls.

We live in a mechanical world, and we live in a commercial world. The two questions that seem to control society are "Does it work?" and "Does it pay?" with the emphasis on the latter question. To quote Thoreau again, we have "improved means to unimproved ends." For centuries the philosophers and mystics have been reminding us that we cannot enjoy the things that money can buy if we lose the things money cannot buy. Making a living has replaced making a life, and searching after new schemes and methods has replaced discovering truth and building character. The very fact of wonder demands values, for we do not wonder at that which is cheap and contemptible. When values vanish, wonder must vanish, too.

Our world is a busy world; it has little time to pause, contemplate, and wonder. Even the vacationer pauses only long enough to set his lens and shutter and take several pictures that he can contemplate at home. We do not have time to get close to people or to life. The child lives in a world of wonder because he stands still and watches and ponders. Our lives are so full they are empty. We boast about the quantity of our activity without admitting the lack of quality in our experience. We know how to count, but we do not know how to weigh; and we are the losers in the long run.

Perhaps the greatest cause for the lack of wonder is this—we live in an *artificial* world. Most people are living on substitutes and do not know it. Inane comedy has replaced humor, cheap amusement has replaced wholesome recreation, and propaganda has replaced truth. Millions of bored people depend on manufactured experiences to rescue them from their tedious existence. Each experience must be greater than the previous one, and the result is a nervous system so taxed beyond measure by substitute stimulants that the person finds it harder and harder to recognize and enjoy a true emotional experience. One of the tragic consequences of living on the artificial is a gradual loss of the real.

The greatest substitute of all is sin, and this is what lies at the root of the whole matter. Unless you and I do something about our sins, we are never going to be able to experience and enjoy the wonder that God wants to bring to our lives. The essence of idolatry is worshiping and serving something other than God; living, if you please, on substitutes. But it is a basic law of life that we become like the gods we worship; so, if our god is an artificial substitute, we will become artificial, too. The very senses that ought to thrill us with wonder become jaded, then paralyzed, then dead. "They have mouths, but they speak not: eyes have they, but they see not: they have ears, but they hear not: noses have they, but they smell not.... They that make them [the idols] are like unto them; so is every one that trusteth in them" (Psalm 115:5, 6, 8).

The only Person who can deal with our basic needs and restore wonder to our lives is Jesus Christ, because his name is Wonderful.

The Wonders of Jesus. Why is Jesus Christ called Wonderful?

To name his name is to give the answer; for we would be amazed if he were *not* called Wonderful! Everything about Jesus Christ makes the believing heart say, "I will now turn aside and see this great sight!" He is wonderful in his Person. Imagine God coming to earth as man! *"Christ, by highest heaven adored;/ Christ, the Everlasting Lord!/ Late in time behold Him come,/ Offspring of the Virgin's womb:/ Veiled in flesh the Godhead see;/ Hail th' Incarnate Deity!/ Pleased as man with man to dwell,/ Jesus, our Emmanuel."*

When the shepherds shared the news of the birth of Jesus, "all they that heard it wondered at those things which were told them by the shepherds" (Luke 2:18). It was something to wonder at: "God was manifest in the flesh" (1 Timothy 3:16).

Christ was wonderful in the life he lived on earth. Everything that yielded to him participated in wonder. It was just another wedding until Jesus arrived, and he transformed it into an occasion that is still pondered by devout souls. Ordinary servants put ordinary water into ordinary stone pots and then—*the extraordinary happened!* The wonder of it all—water was turned into wine! But this is the wonder of his life; whatever he touched took on new substance and new meaning. Peter and his fisherman friends would have lived ordinary lives, and died ordinary deaths, had they never met Jesus. Peter had caught fish before he met Jesus; but when Jesus was giving the orders, catching fish was a totally new experience. "Launch out into the deep!" "Cast the net on the right side of the ship!" And Peter had experienced storms on the Sea of Galilee, but the experience was different when Jesus Christ was in control. "Peace! Be still!" Jesus even let Peter walk on the water!

Whatever Jesus touched, he blessed and beautified and made wonderful. He tried to open men's eyes to see the world around them: the splendor of the lilies, the freedom of the sparrows, the miracle of the children. He took everyday bread and wine and gave these necessities a depth of meaning that transformed them into luxuries of God's grace. A little seed suddenly becomes a sermon: "The seed is the Word of God." Water is a picture of the Holy Spirit. A lost sheep is a lost soul. He wrote in the dust and confounded the angry religious leaders. Perhaps the greatest wonder of all, he transformed a shameful cross into the meeting place of God's love and man's sin.

Everything about Jesus is wonderful—his birth, his life, his words. "And all bare him witness, and wondered at the gracious words which proceeded out of his mouth" (Luke 4:22). Unlike the scribes, who quoted authorities, Jesus spoke with authority. His was no second-hand tradition; his message was firsthand truth from God. "I speak to the world those things which I have heard of him" (John 8:26). And he practiced what he taught! "Which of you convinceth me of sin?" (John 8:46). In his words we find simplicity—the common people heard him gladly—and yet profundity, a depth of meaning that the greatest minds are still trying to fathom. He was at home with the lowliest peasant or the most learned rabbi. The greatest wonder of his teaching is that in his words we have life. "The words that I speak unto you, they are spirit, and they are life" (John 6:63). We read the greatest writings of the ages and our hearts are stirred and our minds are enlightened; but we meditate on the words of Christ, and we share in the wonder of life. They feed the inner man. They give much more than enlightenment—they give *enablement*, they enable us to live.

Consider the wonder of his death. He came to die; he knew he was going to die; he was willing to die. If any man ever had a right to live, it was Jesus Christ; yet he willingly died, "even the death of the cross."

"Well might the sun in darkness hide,/ And shut His glories in,/ When Christ the mighty Maker died/ For man the creature's sin." Far greater than the three hours of darkness, or the earthquake that rent the tombs, was the loving surrender of the Son of God as he willingly bore the sins of the world in his own body. What wondrous love is this! And add to this the wonder of his resurrection and his ascension. Add further the wonder of the salvation that he purchased for us! Oh, my soul! What a wonder he is!

The Wonder of Jesus in Me. How can you and I share in this wonder? Do we even *need* wonder in our lives? Yes, we do; otherwise life becomes bland and blind, dull and dead, and we miss much of what God has prepared for us. The dullness of life is not caused by circumstances on the outside, but by spiritual conditions on the inside. Jesus lived in the same world as the multitudes

that followed him, and yet it was not the
same world—it was a different and
more wonderful world. "They seeing see
not; and hearing they hear not, neither do
they understand" (Matthew 13:13).
Whenever he spoke about deeper
spiritual realities, they thought he meant
material, surface things. "Destroy this
temple, and in three days I will raise it
up!" They thought he meant the Jewish
Temple, but "he spake of the temple of
his body" (John 2:19-21). "Ye must be
born again!" "How can a man be born
when he is old?" Nicodemus thought
of physical birth, but our Lord was
speaking of spiritual birth. It was truly
night for Nicodemus—he could not see.
The woman at the well thought Jesus
was speaking of physical water; the
crowds in John 6 thought he was speaking
about literally eating his flesh and
drinking his blood. Oh, the blindness
of those who have no wonder in their
hearts!

Wonder is important; his name
"Wonderful" leads the list. Unless I
know something of his wonder, I can
never come to him for counsel, or for
power, or for any other spiritual essential.
Wonder leads to worship, and worship
to growth, and growth to character and
service. Wonder begins with receiving
Christ into the heart and life,
experiencing the forgiveness of sins and
the invasion of a whole new life.
"Christ liveth in me" (Galatians 2:20). "I
will come in to him, and will sup with

him, and he with me" (Revelation 3:20).

When you are born again into God's family, you receive a whole new set of spiritual senses, and the inner person is raised from the dead and given divine life. *"Heav'n above is softer blue,/ Earth around is sweeter green!/ Something lives in every hue/ Christless eyes have never seen:/ Birds with gladder songs o'erflow,/ Flow'rs with deeper beauty shine,/ Since I know, as now I know,/ I am His, and He is mine."*

Wonder comes to your life as you walk with him in obedience and consecration. How much the disciples learned as they listened to him, walked with him, and let him guide their lives! There is no substitute for daily fellowship with the Lord in his Word and in prayer, and then walking with him in obedience. This kind of daily experience sharpens the spiritual senses of the inner man. Your eyes begin to see what he sees; your ears hear what he hears; and (most important of all) your heart begins to love what he loves. Your values change as your vision sharpens. Your deepening love for Christ opens new windows and doors for you, and life begins to fulfil the promise of 1 Corinthians 2:9—"Eye hath not seen, nor ear heard, neither have entered into the heart of man, the things which God hath prepared for them that love him." Wonder is a liberating experience; it breaks the shackles and calls us to a life of faith and love.

This life of wonder with the
Wonderful One climaxes in glory: "We
know that, when he shall appear, we shall
be like him; for we shall see him as he
is" (1 John 3:2). Eternal wonder! Seeing
with perfect vision—loving with sinless
hearts—obeying with wills that are lost in
the wonder of the glory of God! The
glory of heaven is its wonder in Christ;
the tragedy of hell is the absence of
wonder. Darkness ... dullness ...
frightening monotony ... eternal
loneliness ... eternal purposelessness ...
this is hell. Pain, yes; judgment, yes; but
permeating it all, that awful dullness of
man's sins when that first pleasure is
gone. *To be forsaken by God means
that the wonder is taken out of your life
for all eternity.* Jesus called hell
"Gehenna," referring to the garbage
dump burning outside Jerusalem. What
a tragedy—man ceases to be man and
ends up just a piece of junk, a cast-off
thing, on an eternal garbage heap!

Those who walk with Christ by faith
know the meaning of wonder in their
daily lives. Ordinary people experience
extraordinary things because of the
wonder of Christ. These wonders may
not be obvious to those outside the
family of God, but they are clearly visible
to those inside the family. His wonders
are seen in so-called little things, such
as a flower, or a bird, or a baby's smile.
And they are seen in big things, such as
the courage to say "No" or the strength
to keep going when the road is

difficult. Little things become big things when they are touched with the wonder of Christ.

He can make your life wonderful because his name is—Wonderful.

His name is
COUNSELLOR
This takes care of the
decisions of life.
*Thou shalt guide me
with thy counsel,
and afterward receive me
to glory.*
PSALM 73:24

THREE
COUNSELLOR

Where people turn for help is some indication of their character and faith. One man turns to the local bar where he pours out his troubles into the ears of those he thinks are concerned friends. Another person visits a "reader" or a fortune-teller, or perhaps pays to have his horoscope cast. More sensible people talk their problems over with a doctor or pastor, or perhaps visit a psychologist or other trained counsellor.

To the Christian, Jesus Christ is the supreme Counsellor. "Lord, to whom shall we go? thou hast the words of eternal life" (John 6:68). The fact that he is called "Counsellor" reveals several important truths to us.

The Necessity of God's Counsel. You and I need counsel; and Jesus Christ is the Counsellor—he is to us all that we need. "O Lord," cried Jeremiah, "I know that the way of man is not in himself: it is not in man that walketh to direct his steps" (10:23). Why you and I have a difficult time directing our steps is not hard to understand. To begin with, man's heart is basically sinful and selfish, and his motives are mixed. Jeremiah says it accurately: "The heart is deceitful above all things, and desperately wicked: who can know it?" (17:9). How easy it is to say, "Well, if I know my own heart—" and then have to confess that we do *not* know our own hearts. Peter looked into his heart and thought he saw courage and stability; Jesus looked into that same heart and saw cowardice and failure. "Counsel in the heart of man is like deep water," warns Proverbs 20:5.

Not only is the heart selfish, but the mind is severely limited. "For my thoughts are not your thoughts, neither are your ways my ways, saith the Lord" (Isaiah 55:8). After conversion, the mind of the believer has to be *transformed* so that he might "prove what is that good, and acceptable, and perfect, will of God" (Romans 12:2). The mind of man is an amazing machine for understanding knowledge, but it is greatly limited when it comes to grasping spiritual wisdom. Even Peter could not understand why Jesus had to die on a cross!

Added to the internal deficiencies—a selfish heart and a limited mind—are the external problems: the pressures of the world and the devices of the devil.

"Blessed is the man that walketh not in the counsel of the ungodly" (Psalm 1:1). "Be not conformed to this world..." (Romans 12:2). We are surrounded by ungodly thinking and anti-God thinking, and if we are not careful, it will influence us in the decisions we make. "He to whom the Eternal Word speaketh," wrote Thomas à Kempis, "is delivered from a world of unnecessary conceptions." Imagine, if you will, a physician treating a patient and having no knowledge of modern drugs or surgical techniques! Imagine an African witch doctor practicing at Mayo Clinic! "As he thinketh ... so is he" (Proverbs 23:7).

Satan blinds the minds of unbelievers (2 Corinthians 4:1-4) and seeks to deceive the minds of believers (2 Corinthians 11:1-3); he also tries to use the unbelievers to lead the believers astray. The thing that plunged mankind into sin was the deceiving of Eve's mind, and ever since that event, the mind of man has been at variance with God and at enmity with God. No matter how we assess the situation, you and I desperately need God's counsel if we are to make a success of life to the glory of God.

The giving of counsel to his children is one of God's most gracious works. The very way he does it is an evidence of his love and kindness. "If any of you lack wisdom, let him ask of God, that giveth to all men liberally, and does not scold; and it shall be given him" (James 1:5, literal translation). Some people would want a complete guidebook that they could consult for direction—rules to obey and laws to follow—but God does not counsel us in that way. If he did, we would remain immature children and never grow to be more like Christ. I was driving to Canada one summer, and the local automobile club gave me a book of information that outlined the entire trip. It told me the roads to take, the restaurants to eat at, and even the "police traps" to watch out for along the way! This may be fine for a vacation trip, but it will never do on the road of life. God gives us a compass and a Book of promises and principles—the Bible—and lets us make our decisions day by day as we sense the leading of his Spirit. *This is how we grow.* Being forced to come to Christ, our Counsellor, matures us, strengthens us, and brings more glory to God.

The fact that Jesus Christ is the Counsellor indicates that he has a definite plan for each life. We are not left to drift or to wander, for he knows where we ought to be and what we ought to do. When we seek for counsel, we are not asking for a luxury; we are seeking a necessity. We must have the guidance of God if we are to experience the grace of God and manifest the glory of God.

Christ—Qualified Counsellor. Since Jesus Christ is called "Counsellor," it

means that he is qualified to counsel us.
Not every person is so qualified; in fact,
it is against the law to advertise your
services as a counsellor unless you
possess the necessary credentials.
Having an interest in people and being
able to give advice are not sufficient
credentials in most states. They require a
certain amount of education, some
practical experience under the
guidance of a trained counsellor, and
proficiency in the field as proved by
official examinations.

Is Jesus Christ qualified to be your
Counsellor? Of course, he is!

For one thing, he is eternal God in
whom "dwelleth all the fulness of the
Godhead bodily" (Colossians 2:9).
Jesus Christ was a part of the eternal
counsel of creation. He was there when
the Father said, "Let us make man!"
Solomon's "Hymn to Wisdom" in
Proverbs 8:22-36 reminds us of Jesus
Christ, the eternal Son of God, and Paul
tells us that in Christ "are hid all the
treasures of wisdom and knowledge"
(Colossians 2:3). There is nothing that he
does not know!

But something else makes him a
qualified counsellor—he *is also man*.
Because he was born into this world,
grew up, labored, suffered, and
died, he is able to enter into the
experiences that perplex and burden
you. How many times the professional
counsellor hears, "Oh, you just don't
understand!" But those words can never

honestly be spoken to Jesus Christ, because he does understand. "And it was necessary for Jesus to be like us, his brothers, so that he could be our merciful and faithful High Priest before God.... For since he himself has now been through suffering and temptation, he knows what it is like when we suffer and are tempted, and he is wonderfully able to help us" (Hebrews 2:17, 18, *The Living Bible*).

Consider another fact—*he loves us*. Counsellors are warned not to get involved emotionally with their patients, lest this involvement hinder them from doing their best. But Jesus Christ always speaks the truth in love (Ephesians 4:15). In the Upper Room, he told Peter the truth about himself, and tried to guide Peter into the place of victory. Unfortunately, Peter rejected the truth, and even argued with it; the result was shameful failure. Some people hold back the truth because they think this is one way to show love. Others tell the truth but have no love. Jesus Christ is able to blend both truth and love, and this makes him an effective Counsellor.

As our Counsellor, Jesus *encourages us*. "Let not your heart be troubled!" Why wouldn't their hearts be troubled? He had just told them that Peter would deny him and that one of their number was a traitor! On top of this, he had told them that he was leaving them to go back to the Father. Their hearts *were* troubled, deeply so; and so he sought to encourage them and prepare them for the demands that lay before them. He told them about the Father's house. He told them about the Holy Spirit, the "Comforter," the "Encourager" (for that is what the word *comfort* really means). A good counsellor does not *protect* us from the problems of life; instead, he *prepares* us for life's problems and helps us face them honestly and courageously. "God is our refuge and strength, a very present help in trouble" (Psalm 46:1). As our refuge, he hides us; as our strength, he helps us. We do not leave our Counsellor merely with good advice; he sends us away with the strength we need to do what he tells us to do.

Jesus Christ, our Counsellor, is *patient with us.* As you read the four Gospels, you are impressed with our Lord's patience with his disciples as he answers their questions, endures their ignorance and selfishness, and attempts to teach them and prepare them for their life's ministry. Even the best counsellor occasionally loses patience and tries to push his client faster than he is able to go, but not so with the Lord Jesus Christ. "I have yet many things to say unto you, but ye cannot bear them now" (John 16:12). He knows the right time and the right circumstances for revealing a new truth or reminding us of an old truth.

Our heavenly Counsellor *knows our*

hearts. "He knew all men, and needed not that any should testify of man: for he knew what was in man" (John 2:24, 25). "And all the churches shall know that I am he who searches deep within men's hearts, and minds..." (Revelation 2:23, *The Living Bible*). "Counsel in the heart of man is like deep water; but a man of understanding will draw it out" (Proverbs 20:5). To a human counsellor we may say, "Sir, thou hast nothing to draw with, and the well is deep" (John 4:11); but we could never make that statement to Jesus Christ. He knows the human heart and mind, and he is able to help us understand ourselves. What a wonderful Counsellor!

I would add one final characteristic that shows the greatness of our Counsellor—*he prays for us.* "Neither pray I for these alone, but for them also which shall believe on me through their word" (John 17:20). He prays for us constantly, for "he ever liveth to make intercession for them" (Hebrews 7:25). For what does he pray? That we might be made "perfect in every good work to do his will" (Hebrews 13:21). "For it is God which worketh in you, both to will and to do of his good pleasure" (Philippians 2:13).

You and I need spiritual counsel, and Jesus Christ is perfectly qualified to be our Counsellor.

His Counsel in Our Lives. Christ's counsel is available to us now. Providing this counsel is a part of his ministry as our High Priest.

He counsels us through his Word. "Thy testimonies also are my delight and my counsellors" (Psalm 119:24). The margin reads, "and the men of my counsel." Consider the wisdom that God gives us through his Word. "Thou through thy commandments hast made me wiser than mine enemies ... I have more understanding than all my teachers ... I understand more than the ancients..." (Psalm 119:98-100). We can learn from the Word what other people must learn in battles or books, or in the difficult "school of hard knocks." There is no need for the Christian to "learn the hard way" by suffering the bitter consequences of sin. We can learn from the Word, avoid sin, and be the wiser for it.

He also counsels us by his Spirit. "And the spirit of the Lord shall rest upon him, the spirit of wisdom and understanding, the spirit of counsel and might" (Isaiah 11:2). The Spirit of God teaches us from the Word of God. He also teaches us in the everyday experiences of life as he speaks to us and directs us. "Now when they had gone throughout Phrygia and the region of Galatia, and were forbidden of the Holy Ghost to preach the Word in Asia, after they were come to Mysia, they assayed to go into Bithynia: but the Spirit suffered them not" (Acts 16:6, 7). How the Holy Spirit directed Paul and his party, we do not know; but that he does direct us, we can be sure.

Often the Lord uses circumstances to give us counsel and direction. "I will instruct thee and teach thee in the way which thou shalt go: I will guide thee with mine eye" (Psalm 32:8). "I will counsel you with my eye upon you," reads the *New American Standard Bible.* What *human* counsellor can keep his eye upon his counselee to make sure that he obeys? "For the eyes of the Lord are over the righteous, and his ears are open unto their prayers" (1 Peter 3:12). The child of God learns that his Father is in control of circumstances, and that the things that happen often point the way to the will of God.

Our Counsellor will often use people to help direct us. "Ointment and perfume rejoice the heart: so doth the sweetness of a man's friend by hearty counsel" (Proverbs 27:9). This is one of the blessings of Christian fellowship in the local gathering of believers—we are able to encourage and admonish one another in the will of God. We must be careful, of course, to listen to *wise* counsellors. King Rehoboam listened to his young friends, and the results for him and the kingdom were tragic.

So our Counsellor directs us by his Word, his Spirit, the circumstances of life, and the believers with whom we fellowship. But what must *we* do that this counsel might come to us? First of all, and most important, *we must be*

willing to do what he says. "If any of you
really determines to do God's will, then
you will certainly know whether my
teaching is from God or is merely my
own" (John 7:17, *The Living Bible*). God
does not give his counsel to the curious
or the careless; he reveals his will to the
concerned and the consecrated. Some
believers take the attitude, "I'll ask God
what he wants me to do, and if I like it,
I'll do it." The result is predictable: God
does not speak to them. Unless we have
a serious desire to know and to *do* the
counsel of God, he will not reveal his
will to us.

We must *seek God's counsel.* "My son,
if thou wilt receive my words, and hide
my commandments with thee; so that
thou incline thine ear unto wisdom,
and apply thine heart to understanding;
yea, if thou criest after knowledge, and
liftest up thy voice for understanding; if
thou seekest her as silver, and searchest
for her as for hid treasures; then shalt
thou understand the fear of the Lord, and
find the knowledge of God" (Proverbs
2:1-5). Sad to say, many times people
have come to me for spiritual counsel
without a desire to seek the mind and will
of God. They were impatient; they
wanted me to hand them a
pre-packaged plan. They were unwilling
to discipline themselves in Bible study
and prayer to diligently seek the wisdom
God had for them. They expected to
find nuggets of truth lying on the surface

of life, and were unwilling to dig for the hidden treasures.

Desire God's counsel, seek it, *and wait for it*. This unwillingness to wait on the Lord was what led Israel into disobedience time after time. "They soon forgat his works; they waited not for his counsel" (Psalm 106:13). A teacher can instruct a pupil in algebra and answer his questions immediately; but in the school of life, our Counsellor must wait until we are ready for the answer. "I have yet many things to say unto you, but ye cannot bear them now" (John 16:12). God's delays are preparation for God's blessings. If you do not know what God wants you to do, wait and keep doing the last thing he told you to do. Your gracious Counsellor will never lead you astray, but you can lead yourself astray if you become impatient and impulsive. "He that believeth shall not make haste" (Isaiah 28:16).

When he shows you his counsel, *accept it*. Do not argue with it; do not ask him to revise it; simply accept it. God's will is not given to us for our approval; it is given for our acceptance. There is no "money-back guarantee" if we are not completely satisfied. We must accept God's will, and then *obey it*. The blessing does not come in the discovery of God's will, but in the doing of God's will. God's standard is "doing the will of God from the heart" (Ephesians 6:6).

Your Counsellor knows the many decisions you must make, and he knows how important those decisions are to you— and to him. God is eternally wrapped up in your life; he has a tremendous investment in you and your future. He has more to lose if you fail than you do, for his eternal glory is at stake. He wants to be your Counsellor and show you his will. He does not want to counsel you only in the emergencies of life; He wants to counsel you every day in even the mundane things of life. "Whether therefore ye eat, or drink, or whatsoever ye do, do all to the glory of God" (1 Corinthians 10:31). As you seek his counsel, you get to know him better; and in knowing him better, you understand his will better. God's counsel cannot be separated from God's character; his Person and his plan must go together, for "he cannot deny himself" (2 Timothy 2:13). The more two persons love each other, the more they involve each other in the plans and activities of life. Your Counsellor wants to be a part of every area of your life.

God does not need our counsel; we need his. "For who hath known the mind of the Lord? or who hath been his counsellor?" (Romans 11:34). Too often we come to him and tell him what he ought to do! Instead, we need to wait before him and let him counsel us. "Speak, Lord; for thy servant heareth" (1 Samuel 3:9). "This is the way, walk ye in it" (Isaiah 30:21).

There is no need to fear the decisions of life when you know Jesus Christ, for his name is Counsellor.

His name is
THE MIGHTY GOD
This takes care of the
demands of life.
*For he that is mighty
hath done to me
great things....*
LUKE 1:49

FOUR

THE MIGHTY GOD

The history of mankind has been the story of discovering and using power. First it was man power, then horsepower, then steam power, and now atomic power. Each step has enriched mankind materially and financially, but it is doubtful that we are any richer spiritually. Man is able to harness the powers of the universe, but he cannot control himself. Man is still a weakling when it comes to the things that matter most. Some future historian is certain to call the last half of the twentieth century "The Age of Power and Weakness."

The basic power needed today is *spiritual power,* and the source of that power is Jesus Christ; for he is "The mighty God."

Immanuel. The fact that Jesus Christ is called "The mighty God" indicates that *he is God.* Leo Tolstoy wrote: "I believe Christ was a man like ourselves; to look upon him as God would seem to me the greatest of sacrileges." And yet Jesus claimed to be God. He dared to say, "That all men should honour the Son, even as they honour the Father. He that honoureth not the Son honoureth not the Father which hath sent him" (John 5:23). At the close of his sermon on the Good Shepherd, he said boldly, "I and my Father are one" (John 10:30). The people present understood this statement to be a clear claim to deity, and they responded by picking up stones to stone him! Near the close of his public ministry, just before the cross, he cried out, "He that believeth on me, believeth not on me, but on him that sent me. And he that seeth me seeth him that sent me" (John 12:44, 45). He told Philip, "He that hath seen me hath seen the Father" (John 14:9). In plain, simple terms, Jesus Christ claimed to be God.

Those who knew him affirmed that he was God. The Apostle John identified Jesus as "the Word" and wrote: "In the beginning was the Word, and the Word was with God, and the Word was God" (John 1:1). Thomas fell before Jesus and exclaimed, "My Lord and my God!" (John 20:28)—and Jesus did not prevent him or correct him. If any man opposed the idea that Jesus of Nazareth was God in the flesh, it was Saul of Tarsus; but when he met Jesus, the zealous rabbi changed his mind and was for the rest of his life a witness to the deity of Jesus

Christ. Paul wrote concerning his nation, Israel, "Whose are the fathers, and of whom as concerning the flesh Christ came, who is over all, God blessed for ever. Amen" (Romans 9:5). Titus 2:13 says, "Looking for that blessed hope, and the glorious appearing of the great God and our Savior Jesus Christ."

A member of a cult that denies the deity of Christ challenged me one day with, "You can't find one verse in the Bible that calls Jesus 'God!' " I turned to Hebrews 1:8: "But unto the Son he saith, Thy throne, O God, is for ever and ever." His only reply was to refer me to another translation that obviously twisted the original language in order to support their false doctrine.

Referring to Jesus Christ, the Apostle John writes: "This is the true God and eternal life" (1 John 5:20). One does not have to be a Greek scholar to understand that statement. Jesus claimed to be God and he accepted the claim from the lips of others. He accepted worship as God. He claimed to do things that only God can do, such as forgive sins.

The names that he bears affirm his deity. The very name "Jesus" means "Jehovah is salvation"; while many people in his time bore that name (in tribute to the great leader Joshua), Jesus actually claimed to live up to it. He said to Zacchaeus, "This day is salvation come to this house..." (Luke 19:9). He forgave the sins of the paralytic, and the religious leaders exclaimed, "Why doth this man thus speak blasphemies? who can forgive sins but God only?" (Mark 2:7). One of his names is "Emmanuel" which means "God with us" (Matthew 1:23). The angel identified him to Mary as "that holy thing which shall be born of thee ... the Son of God" (Luke 1:35). Mary was the one witness who could have saved Jesus from the cross. Yet she stood at the cross and made no protest. *If Jesus was not God, why was Mary silent?*

Since he is God, he deserves our faith, love, obedience, service, and worship. "He is thy Lord; and worship thou him" (Psalm 45:11). To reject Christ is to reject God, and to reject God is to reject life. "He that believeth on the Son hath everlasting life: and he that believeth not the Son shall not see life; but the wrath of God abideth on him" (John 3:36). "After six years given to the impartial investigation of Christianity," wrote General Lew Wallace, author of *Ben Hur*, "as to its truth or falsity, I have come to the deliberate conclusion that Jesus Christ was the Messiah of the Jews, the Savior of the world, and my personal Savior." Jesus cannot be avoided; we must face him and decide. Isaiah says that he is God. What do you say?

Christ's Power Revealed. Not only is Jesus called God, but he is called "The *mighty* God." What a paradox that a babe in a manger should be called *mighty*! Yet even as a baby, Jesus Christ revealed

power. His birth affected the heavens as
that star appeared. The star affected the
Magi, and they left their homes and
made that long journey to Jerusalem.
Their announcement shook King Herod
and his court. Jesus' birth brought angels
from heaven and simple shepherds
from their flocks on the hillside.
Midnight became midday as the glory of
the Lord appeared to men.

We also see the mighty power of
Jesus Christ in the creation of the
universe. "All things were made by him;
and without him was not any thing
made that was made" (John 1:3).
Obviously, then, he himself was not
created since he made everything that was
made. No statement in Scripture puts it
more majestically than Hebrews 1:1-3:
"God, who at sundry times and in divers
manners spake in times past unto the
fathers by the prophets, hath in these last
days spoken unto us by his Son, whom
he hath appointed heir of all things, by
whom also he made the worlds; who
being the brightness of his glory, and the
express image of his person, and
upholding all things by the word of his
power, when he had by himself purged
our sins, sat down on the right hand of the
Majesty on high."

The Apostle Paul agrees with this
statement. "Who is the image of the
invisible God, the firstborn of every
creature: for by him were all things
created, that are in heaven, and that are
in earth, visible and invisible ... all things

were created by him, and for him" (Colossians 1:15, 16). What mystery—the Creator becomes a creature! He who fills all things becomes an infant in a cattle stall! The mighty God!

Not only does Jesus reveal his power in creation, but also in history. The Bethlehem promise tells us this: "But thou, Bethlehem Ephratah, though thou be little among the thousands of Judah, yet out of thee shall he come forth unto me that is to be ruler in Israel; whose goings forth have been from old, from everlasting" (Micah 5:2).

The entire Old Testament history is the story of his goings forth. As Dr. A. T. Pierson used to put it, "History is his story." No matter where you turn in the Old Testament record, you meet Jesus Christ. "Your father Abraham rejoiced to see my day," said Jesus to the Jewish leaders, "and he saw it, and was glad" (John 8:56). Moses accomplished what he did because he esteemed "the reproach of Christ greater riches than the treasures in Egypt" (Hebrews 11:26). Before conquering the city of Jericho, Joshua met Jesus one night and bowed before him in worship (Joshua 5:13-15). The three Hebrew children walked with him in the fiery furnace (Daniel 3:24, 25). No wonder the Lord Jesus was able to teach those discouraged Emmaus disciples from the Old Testament, for it records his goings forth, "And beginning at Moses and all the prophets, he expounded unto them in all the scriptures the things concerning himself" (Luke 24:27).

When he was here on earth, he revealed himself as "The mighty God" by the miracles that he performed. The very accomplishment of these works was evidence of his deity and left the beholders without excuse. "Then began he to upbraid the cities wherein most of his mighty works were done, because they repented not" (Matthew 11:20). His fellow countrymen marveled "that even such mighty works are wrought by his hands" (Mark 6:2). And yet they failed to trust him. "And he could there do no mighty work, save that he laid his hands upon a few sick folk, and healed them" (Mark 6:5). His enemies argued that his power came from Satan; but that was only an evasion of facts, and he quickly demolished their argument. "And if Satan cast out Satan, he is divided against himself; how shall then his kingdom stand?" (Matthew 12:26).

Of course, the greatest act of power that he performed involved his death and resurrection. Paul prayed for the Ephesians (and for us) that they might know "what is the exceeding greatness of his power to us-ward who believe, according to the working of his mighty power, which he wrought in Christ, when he raised him from the dead, and set him at his own right hand in the heavenly places" (Ephesians 1:19, 20).

God raised Jesus from the dead "having loosed the pains of death: because it was not possible that he should be holden of it" (Acts 2:24).

Not only did the Father raise Jesus from the dead, but *Jesus raised himself from the dead!* Speaking of his life, Jesus said, "I have power to lay it down, and I have power to take it again" (John 10:18). "For as the Father hath life in himself, so hath he given to the Son to have life in himself" (John 5:26). This miracle, of course, is centered in his work of redemption—"...Christ died for our sins according to the scriptures; and that he was buried, and that he rose again the third day according to the scriptures" (1 Corinthians 15:3, 4). His resurrection guarantees our redemption. "In whom we have redemption through his blood, the forgiveness of sins, according to the riches of his grace" (Ephesians 1:7).

It is unfortunate that most of the pictures we draw of Jesus (none of which is authentic) depict him as something less than a man. Certainly he was meek, but meekness is not weakness. Meekness is power under control. He was lowly in heart, but he was able to get angry and make a whip of cords and cleanse the temple. His arrest and crucifixion appear to be experiences of weakness, and in one sense they are; but in a deeper sense, they reveal his mighty power. "For though he was crucified through weakness, yet he liveth by the power of

God" (2 Corinthians 13:4). No wonder
Paul shouts, "I can do all things through
Christ which strengtheneth me"
(Philippians 4:13).

Jesus Christ is God, and he is "The
mighty God."

What does this mean to us today who
believe in him?

God's Power in Us. His mighty power
is available to us today. Here is the way
Paul prays for people like us: "For this
cause we also, since the day we heard it,
do not cease to pray for you, and to
desire that ye might be filled with the
knowledge of his will in all wisdom and
spiritual understanding; that ye might
walk worthy of the Lord unto all
pleasing, being fruitful in every
good work, and increasing in
the knowledge of God; strengthened
with all might, according to his
glorious power, unto all patience and
longsuffering with joyfulness"
(Colossians 1:9-11).

Note the universals in that prayer: all
wisdom, all pleasing, every good work,
all might. If God fills us with "all might,"
then that makes us *almighty!*
Strengthened with all might! We have
no problem believing that Jesus Christ is
almighty, but to assign this attribute to his
people—mere creatures of clay—is a
great leap of faith. But it is true—the
almighty power of God is available to us
through Jesus Christ.

Salvation is not something that God
begins and we finish. Salvation is

God's work from start to finish. "Being confident of this very thing, that he which hath begun a good work in you will perform it [complete it] until the day of Jesus Christ" (Philippians 1:6). On the cross, Jesus cried, "It is finished!" *He provides a complete salvation.* He did not make the down payment and expect us to keep up the installments! It is finished!

This means that every believer can claim from Christ all that he needs. "But my God shall supply all your needs according to his riches in glory by Christ Jesus" (Philippians 4:19). But note that Paul's prayer in Colossians 1 deals with the *inner* man, the character of the believer, and not simply material or physical things: "Strengthened with all might ... unto all patience and longsuffering with joyfulness." The almighty power of God is available to us through Jesus Christ that we might develop Christian character and practice Christian conduct to the glory of God. Patience—longsuffering—joyfulness— it takes spiritual power to produce this kind of fruit in our lives.

Paul himself is a good example of what the power of God can do in a life. Paul had a thorn in the flesh (2 Corinthians 12:7-10). What it was, we do not know, but we know that it was severe enough for him to pray three times that God might take it away. Paul's prayer seems logical. After all, he was an important man with a great work to do, and physical pain and weakness would only hinder his ministry. As you read Paul's account of this experience, you detect several levels of spiritual understanding. First, Paul tried to *escape* the thorn; but God refused to remove it. Then Paul *endured* the thorn, but that was not the level that glorified God the most. Even an unsaved person can courageously endure pain. God's grace moved Paul to a higher level—he accepted his pain, then learned to *enjoy* it! "Most gladly therefore will I rather glory in my infirmities, that the power of Christ may rest upon me" (verse 9). He learned to be enriched and empowered by the weakness that his handicap brought to his life. The secret? "My grace is sufficient for thee: for my strength is made perfect in weakness" (verse 9).

The grace of God brings the power of God to our lives. Paul confesses it openly: "But by the grace of God I am what I am" (1 Corinthians 15:10). God's grace is channeled to our lives through God's Son, Jesus Christ. "And of his fulness have all we received, and grace for grace" (John 1:16). Through grace God does in and through us what we cannot do for ourselves. Grace is not simply a supplement to our strength, for we have no strength of our own. Grace turns our weakness into power for the glory of God. "For when I am weak, then am I strong" (2 Corinthians 12:10). The reason many people do not experience

God's power is because they are too strong in themselves. God has to wait until they are weak; then he can share his power with them.

The Bible contains many examples of this principle of weakness turned into strength. When Abraham was seventy-five years old, God promised to give him a son through whom a great nation would be built and the whole world blessed. Ten years went by, and the son had not yet been given. Abraham's wife Sarah suggested that he take her handmaid, Hagar, and have a son by her, and Abraham cooperated with the plan. Hagar did bear a son, but the whole thing was out of God's will and led to great problems. God waited another thirteen years, until Abraham was ninety-nine years old, before he began to fulfil his promise. And when Abraham was 100 years old, and his wife 90, the son was born. Romans 4:19-21 explains the miracle: "And being not weak in faith, he considered not his own body now dead, when he was about an hundred years old, neither yet the deadness of Sarah's womb: he staggered not at the promise of God through unbelief; but was strong in faith, giving glory to God; and being fully persuaded that, what he had promised, he was able also to perform."

It was Abraham's *faith* that released the power of God. He did not look at circumstances or depend on personal feelings. He simply claimed the almighty power of God—and God raised him and his wife from the dead! God's promises and God's performances go together. "There hath not failed one word of all his good promise" (1 Kings 8:56).

What God did for Abraham and Sarah he also did for Moses, Gideon, David, Daniel, Peter, Paul, and myriads of believing people in the pages of the Bible and in the pages of church history. God worked in them and through them, and they did exploits and brought glory to Christ. God is still looking for believing people who can mediate his almighty power in a world that is characterized by weakness. "For the eyes of the Lord run to and fro throughout the whole earth, to shew himself strong in the behalf of them whose heart is perfect toward him" (2 Chronicles 16:9). A perfect heart does not mean a sinless heart, for no man alive has a sinless heart. It means a heart completely trusting in the Lord, a heart that is not divided. God does not trust his power to those who will not trust him completely.

Whatever may be your burden or battle today, God has the power to meet it, handle it, solve it, and use it for your good and his glory. Jesus Christ is "The mighty God" and his power is available to you. "Now unto him that is able to do exceeding abundantly above all that we ask or think, according to the power that worketh in us..." (Ephesians 3:20).

Admit your own weakness, yield
to him by faith, and receive his power
by faith.

His name is
THE EVERLASTING FATHER
This takes care of the
dimensions of life.
*I am come that they might
have life, and that they
might have it more abundantly.*
JOHN 10:10

FIVE
THE EVERLASTING FATHER

That Jesus Christ the Son of God should be called "The everlasting Father" seems a mystery. If he is the Son, he cannot be the Father, since each Person in the Godhead is separate from the other Persons, yet equally God. God the Father is God, God the Son is God, and God the Spirit is God; but the Father is not the Spirit and the Son is not the Father.

The answer, of course, is in the Jewish use of the word "Father." To an Old Testament Jew reading Isaiah's prophecy, the word "Father" would mean "originator of" or "author of." Jesus called Satan the "father of lies" in John 8:44. Jabal was the "father of such as dwell in tents, and of such as have cattle," according to Genesis 4:20. So in calling Jesus Christ "The everlasting Father," the prophet is saying, "He is the Father of that which is everlasting. He is the Father—Originator—of eternity!"

Eternity! Here is a concept so vast that the human mind cannot grasp it. God is eternal—he has neither beginning nor end. Man has a beginning, but no end. Man will live forever either with God or apart from God, either in eternal glory or eternal darkness. When you trust Jesus Christ, you become a part of eternity! He "fathers" eternity in your life, and this involves much more than simply forgiving your sins. You become a part of the very spiritual life of God. Because Jesus Christ is "Wonderful," he takes care of the dullness of life. As the "Counsellor," he handles the decisions of life. "The mighty God" enables you to meet the demands of life. And "The everlasting Father" provides new dimensions to your life. You become a part of eternity.

Made for Eternity. God made us for eternity. "He has made everything appropriate in its time. He has also set eternity in their heart, without which men will not find out the work which God has done from the beginning even to the end" (Ecclesiastes 3:11, *New American Standard Bible,* see margin). This verse seems to suggest that God so made man's heart that man is dissatisfied with life on the surface and has a deep craving for that which is essential and eternal. Psalm 90 is one expression of man's frustration with time. Man knows that there is something more than this brief physical life, that he is made for something greater than time, and man searches for this missing dimension. In one sense, all of man's quests in science, philosophy, exploration, and even religion are evidences of this deep thirst for the eternal. How many people have died yearning for another lifetime in which to accomplish what they wanted to do! Like the architect of British colonialism in South Africa, Cecil Rhodes, they die saying, "So much left undone!"

Yes, we were made for eternity, and we cannot be truly happy and satisfied until we are sharing in eternity. Life is swift and life is brief, and a man of depth always wants to accomplish more. How you solve this tension between time and eternity determines your philosophy of life and your religious faith. Some people do away with eternity and the God of eternity and live only for time. But then they lose depth and inspiration, because they know that a creature like man is made for something grander than three score years and ten. If this philosophy is taken to its logical limits, it leads to, "Eat, drink, and be merry, for tomorrow we die!" If there is no God and no eternity, then why bother to make the most of today? Get it over with as quickly as possible!

Is there any solution to this tension between time and eternity? Yes, there is, in the Person of Jesus Christ.

When Eternity Invaded Time. God created us for eternity, and Jesus Christ came to earth to reveal eternity. "That which was from the beginning, which we have heard, which we have seen with our eyes, which we have looked upon, and our hands have handled, of the Word of life; (for the life was manifested, and we have seen it, and bear witness, and show unto you that eternal life, which was with the Father, and was manifested unto us)" (1 John 1:1, 2). Certainly the eternal was revealed in creation and in the giving of the Law; but each of those revelations had its handicaps. Creation reveals that there is a God, and that he has power and wisdom, but creation says little or nothing about the love of God and the grace of God. The Law reveals that God is holy and just, and that he desires his people to be holy, but the Law cannot change our hearts. God revealed himself in the events of history and showed his people that he cared, but even here the revelation lacks the personal touch that man so needs.

In sending his Son to earth, God caused eternity to invade time. This was not a temporary visit; when Jesus came, he wedded dust and deity—time and eternity—into one. The eternal Word was made human flesh, and that union will last forever. As the perfect Man here on earth, Jesus Christ showed us what it is like to live by the eternal. He lived as no other lived, and even the publicans and sinners saw that he was different. As you read the four Gospel records, you see the eternal moving in the world of time! Jesus Christ proves that the eternal is real!

Jesus was not simply born; he "came into the world." He invaded time from eternity. His words are "words of eternal life" (John 6:68). His deeds had in them the quality of eternity. He spoke as no man ever spoke, and he lived as no man ever lived. His values were vastly different from those of other religious leaders, and because of this he clashed with the established religious system. Jesus looked at people through the eyes of the eternal and never permitted himself to be shackled by the passing opinions of time. The publicans and sinners were not outcasts to him; they were lost sheep needing the care of a shepherd. He was not impressed with the stones of the Temple, for he was building a temple that would last forever. When he looked at the lily or saw a sparrow fall, he thought of the eternal Father in heaven. Everything Jesus talked about or touched took on a new dimension because he is the "Father of Eternity." Ordinary bread and wine were touched by eternity when Jesus blessed, broke, and shared, saying, "This is my body, broken for you; this cup is the new covenant in my blood." When he rebuked his overzealous disciples and said, "Permit the little children to come to me," he lifted childhood to its highest level. "Except ye be converted and become as little children, ye shall not enter into the kingdom of heaven"

(Matthew 18:3).

God made us for eternity. There is more to life than what meets the eye. In Jesus Christ we see eternity revealed. *He is that eternal life.* But how do you and I experience it? After all, we are—yes, we might as well admit it—sinners. Everything that partakes of sin experiences death. Until you and I can remove this terrible thing called sin, we can never move into the marvelous dimension of the eternal.

When Time and Eternity Met. Jesus came to earth to reveal eternity, and he died that we might share eternal life. "For God so loved the world, that he gave his only begotten Son, that whosoever believeth in him should not perish, but have everlasting life" (John 3:16).

Sin is the great obstacle to experiencing eternal life. Sin is not eternal; only God is eternal. Sin is outside God and therefore produces death, for God is eternal life. Our nature partakes of sin and therefore is a stranger to the eternal. We were created in the image of God, and there is a hunger for eternity in our hearts; but until we do something about our sins, we will never share his eternal life.

God solved the sin problem for us when he sent his Son to die on the cross. *Time and eternity met at Calvary.* Jesus Christ is the Lamb of God "foreordained before the foundation of the world" (1 Peter 1:20) and "slain from the foundation of the world" (Revelation 13:8). God's great plan of salvation was no hasty afterthought; his people were chosen in Christ "before the foundation of the world" (Ephesians 1:4), "according to the eternal purpose which he purposed in Christ Jesus our Lord" (Ephesians 3:11). When Jesus Christ was born at Bethlehem, time and eternity met in a person. When he died at Calvary, time and eternity met in a price, and that price—paid for sin—met the demands of God's holy Law and opened the way for sinners to be forgiven and share in eternity.

Mere religion can never take away sins or give the sinner a share in eternity. Religion is a part of time; we need a Savior who breaks into time from eternity and who is able to take away our sins. We have such a Savior in Jesus Christ. He is "the author of eternal salvation unto all them that obey him" (Hebrews 5:9). By the shedding of his blood, he "obtained eternal redemption for us" (Hebrews 9:12), and he has promised us an "eternal inheritance" (Hebrews 9:15). He gives us the gift of eternal life! "And I give unto them eternal life; and they shall never perish, neither shall any man pluck them out of my hand" (John 10:28).

In order to become the "Father of Eternity" to us, he had to suffer on the cross. Our birth into eternal life required his death. The gift of eternal life was not purchased cheaply.

A Life of Eternity. But Jesus Christ is

the "Father of Eternity" in another way—he lives now to give eternal purpose and quality to our everyday lives. Sin is the great waster; Satan is the great destroyer. Most of the people in the world are existing, not living, and what they live on and live for does not satisfy fully and will not last eternally. Men are living on substitutes, and the substitutes are robbing them of the true experiences of life that God wants them to enjoy. Instead of *investing* time in eternity and enjoying the dividends here and now, most people are *spending* time, or (worse yet) *wasting* time. The person who trusts Jesus Christ will not live for so little.

For the Christian, Jesus Christ is the controller of time. "My times are in thy hand" (Psalm 31:15). Jesus himself lived that way when he was ministering on earth. You cannot read the Gospel of John—a book that magnifies his eternity—without realizing that he lived according to a divine timetable. "Mine hour is not yet come," he said to Mary at the beginning of his ministry (John 2:4). To his brethren he said, "My time is not yet come: but your time is alway ready" (John 7:6). The unbeliever has no divine schedule to follow. When his enemies tried to arrest him, they found it was impossible "because his hour was not yet come" (John 7:30). They wanted to arrest him while he was preaching in the Temple, but they failed, "for his hour was not yet come"

(John 8:20). When Jesus announced that he was returning to Judea because Mary and Martha needed him, his disciples were amazed and afraid. "Master," they protested, "the Jews of late sought to stone thee!" His reply revealed the quiet confidence of his heart in the plan and purpose of the Father: "Are there not twelve hours in the day?" (John 11:9). In other words, "I am not walking by sight, but by faith. My Father has a plan and I will follow it." The climax, of course, came in the Garden when he made that final surrender as he faced the cross: "Father, the hour is come!" (John 17:1).

"My times are in thy hand!" Does God still plan for his own and guide them through life? Yes, he does! Is it reasonable that the God who created time at the beginning should abandon his creation and let it drift like a tramp until the final day of judgment? According to Hebrews 1:2, Jesus Christ "framed the ages" (literal translation). This suggests that even the ages of history are under his control. David looked back and wrote, "I have been young, and now am old; yet have I not seen the righteous forsaken, nor his seed begging bread" (Psalm 37:25). At the end of the pilgrimage, the saints of God have looked back and seen the hand of God at work all their lives. This does not mean that everything they did was in the will of God, or that they never went on detours; but it does mean that God ruled and overruled in their lives to accomplish his eternal purposes.

The fact that Jesus Christ controls time reveals the importance of prayer and the Word of God. As we fellowship with him, he speaks to us and reveals what he wants us to do. *When you pray, you lay hold of eternity.* Your heart and mind become the meeting-place of time and eternity. You can honestly say, "My times are in his hands."

Not only does Jesus Christ control time, but he conquers time. For the unbeliever, time is an enemy; for the dedicated Christian, time is an ally. Jesus Christ entered into time that he might accomplish an eternal purpose. Time became an ally, not an enemy. In our case, eternity enters into us that we might accomplish his purposes in the times that he assigns to us.

How does time fight against people? One way is by *delay*. Men cannot control time. The seconds, minutes, and hours move along at their appointed pace and man can do nothing about it. The child wants to hasten time; the elderly may want to slow it down. The suffering cry out, "How long, O Lord, how long?" Some people, like Peter Pan, want to stop time and remain in the innocent joys of childhood. Others want to speed time along so they can enjoy the pleasures of adulthood. Time is difficult to define, impossible to control.

But the Christian never worries about delay, because his times are in the hands of God. At the wedding of Cana,

Jesus said, "My hour is not yet come." As
he contemplated the sorrow at Bethany,
he said, "Are there not twelve hours in
the day?" In fact, he deliberately delayed
his trip to Bethany! Lazarus had been in
the grave four days by the time Jesus
arrived, but this was in the plan of God.
Jesus went through life unafraid because
his times were in the hands of the Father.
You and I can go through life with this
same confidence, because he has
conquered time.

We need not fear delay, and we need
not fear *decay*, which is time's second
weapon. The hymn-writer wrote,
"Change and decay all around I see."
Change and decay are enemies that most
people fear. Psalm 90 is a vivid
description of the ravages of time as
contrasted with the calm eternity of God.
In his majestic paraphrase of that Psalm,
Isaac Watts writes: *"Time, like an
ever-rolling stream,/ Bears all its sons
away,/ They fly, forgotten, as a dream/
Dies at the op'ning day."*

When we are young, change is a treat;
but as we grow older, change becomes
a threat. But when Jesus Christ is in
control of your life, you need never fear
change or decay. Paul knew this secret
when he wrote: "For our light affliction,
which is but for a moment, worketh for us
a far more exceeding and eternal weight
of glory; while we look not at the things
which are seen, but at the things which are
not seen: for the things which are seen are
temporal; but the things which are not

seen are eternal" (2 Corinthians 4:17, 18).
When you are a part of eternity, the decay
of the material only hastens the
perfecting of the spiritual, if you walk
by faith in Christ.

Time's ultimate weapon is *death*, and
Jesus Christ has conquered there as well.
This is why Paul can shout, "O death,
where is thy sting? O grave, where is
thy victory?" (1 Corinthians 15:55). Man
has invented ways to overcome delay and
decay, but he has yet to defeat death.
Only Jesus Christ can do that. "I am the
resurrection and the life!" he said, and
then he proved it by raising Lazarus from
the grave (John 11:25, 26, 43, 44). In fact,
in that dramatic scene at Bethany, you see
the Lord defeating all three of time's
weapons. He defeated delay by waiting
two days before setting out for Bethany.
By the time he arrived, Lazarus had
begun to decay, so much so that his
sister protested, "Lord, by this time there
will be a stench; for he has been dead
four days" (John 11:39, *New American
Standard Bible*). And he overcame
death, for he raised his friend from the
dead and restored him to his loved ones
again. Jesus Christ conquered time!

He is able to conquer time because he is
the eternal "I Am." He is the "Alpha and
the Omega, the beginning and the end"
(Revelation 21:6). He is timeless and
spaceless; he dwells in eternity. Because
he is above time, he is able to conquer
and control time. Because he entered
into time, he is able to bring eternity into

our little lives and move us into a vast
new dimension of experience. "He that
doeth the will of God abideth forever"
(1 John 2:17). Time flows from the future
(tomorrow) into the present (today) into
the past (yesterday). Only God lives in
the future; man comes out of the past.
The present, then, is the meeting of the
future and the past, and that meeting can
be either triumph or tragedy. When Jesus
Christ is in control of your life, each
moment is an eternal experience because
he gives to you a quality of life that comes
out of eternity. "Eternal life" means
much more than living forever, for even
the lost are going to exist forever. "Eternal
life" means "the life of eternity." It is
an experience in Christ here and now!

Jesus Christ made us for eternity. To
reject him is to miss the very purpose for
which we were created. He came to earth
to reveal eternity, and he died to give
us eternal life. He lives to make eternity
a real experience for us day by day, as he
controls and conquers time. But there is
a final ministry that he performs as
"The Father of Eternity." One day he
will return to take us to a glorious eternal
home.

The End of Time. Salvation from sin
through faith in Christ is not the end; it
is the beginning. The best is yet to come!
"For the Lord himself shall descend
from heaven with a shout, with the voice
of the archangel, and with the
trump of God: and the dead in Christ shall
rise first: then we which are alive and

remain shall be caught up together with them in the clouds, to meet the Lord in the air: and so shall we ever be with the Lord" (1 Thessalonians 4:16, 17). "...in a moment, in the twinkling of an eye, at the last trump: for the trumpet shall sound, and the dead shall be raised incorruptible, and we shall be changed" (1 Corinthians 15:52).

The last change will be the final change. Time will be no more. We shall share in eternity *in our completeness*, with a glorious new body that will know nothing of decay or death. We will live with Christ in the eternal *now*. The lost, sad to say, will be separated from God forever, sharing in eternal decay and death. Such is the tragedy of life without Christ.

As the eternal Holy Spirit works in our lives, we participate in the eternal plan and work of God. As we obey his Word, our lives take on the quality of the eternal. We live *in* time, but we live *for* eternity. "He that doeth the will of God abideth forever" (1 John 2:17). Life is not spent or wasted; life is invested in the eternal. No matter what we experience in life, it is an investment in eternity. The eternal is so glorious that the temporal with its burdens and problems does not defeat us. The outward man is perishing, but the inward man is being renewed day by day.

Jesus Christ is the "Father of Eternity." As your Savior and Lord, let him give birth to the eternal in your life.

His name is
THE PRINCE OF PEACE
This takes care of the
disturbances of life.
Peace I leave with you,
my peace I give unto you.
JOHN 14:27

SIX

THE PRINCE OF PEACE

Like most important words, "peace" has become all things to all men. A loving mother looks upon the face of her sleeping infant and thinks of peace. A poet looks across the headstones in an old graveyard and thinks of peace. Yet who would exchange the potential of a growing infant with the frozen, silent solemnity of a cemetery?

The Old Testament Jew would not make that mistake. To him, the word "peace"—*shalom*—meant far more than silence or the absence of war. Peace was a living, vibrant thing that made for the well-being of mankind. Peace meant (as Dr. George Morrison expresses it) "the possession of adequate resources." It has nothing to do with the situation on the outside; it has everything to do with the condition on the inside. I have seen people sitting in the quiet beauty of nature, where the silence covered everything with a blanket that almost smothered you; and I have watched these people grow restless with inactivity, smoke one cigarette after another, drink one cocktail after another, and complain that they are bored. And I have seen people in the midst of the noisy city, surrounded by the abrasive sounds that only a city can manufacture; and I have watched them smile, and I have heard them sing, and I have recognized that they were at peace.

The difference? Jesus Christ.

Christ Our Peace. When you think of Jesus Christ as "The Prince of Peace," you immediately think of his character. Jesus was a man of peace. You see this as you watch him in the different circumstances of life. He is able to fall asleep in the ship in the midst of a storm so threatening that even his fishermen disciples are terrified. He faces over five thousand hungry people and assures his worried disciples that he knows what he will do. The professional mourners at the home of Jairus laugh in his face when he tells them the little girl is only asleep; but he calmly enters her room and raises her from the dead. Even the two demoniacs in the graveyard of Gadara do not frighten him. Because he is "The Prince of Peace," he is able to bring peace to their divided and distressed hearts. In the Garden, Peter pulls out a sword and declares war; but Jesus calmly faces the mob and peacefully surrenders to be arrested and crucified.

His entire trial is a travesty of justice. Yet Jesus calmly moves from judge to judge, and "...as a lamb to the slaughter, and as a sheep before her shearers is dumb, so he openeth not his mouth" (Isaiah 53:7). Pilate marvels at his silence. While the other prisoners curse their executors, Jesus prays, "Father, forgive them; for they know not what they do" (Luke 23:34). He refuses the narcotic offered him that he might with a clear mind and controlled will accomplish God's eternal purposes on the cross. Who would believe the words of a drugged man? And who would believe that he really suffered to the depths? Our Lord's peace did not come from the absence of trouble or the presence of narcotics. It came from the depths of his soul where he fellowshiped with the Father.

You cannot separate peace and character. What we do depends a great deal on what we are. The secret of our Lord's peace was the Father. As he led his disciples from the Upper Room to the Garden, he said, "But that the world may know that I love the Father; and as the Father gave me commandment, even so I do" (John 14:31). To be sure, Jesus Christ is God in the flesh; but when he was here on earth, he laid aside his own independent use of his divine attributes and lived by faith in the Father. He lived as you and I must live. He loved the Father, and therefore he trusted the

Father; and this gave him peace.

Righteousness and peace go together. "And the work of righteousness shall be peace; and the effect of righteousness quietness and assurance for ever" (Isaiah 32:17). Our Lord's first concern was not peace, but righteousness. "Peace at any price!" was a statement never found on his lips. Peace without righteousness would be victory for the forces of the evil one. Jeremiah wept over this kind of peace: "They have healed also the hurt of the daughter of my people slightly, saying, Peace, peace, when there is no peace" (Jeremiah 6:14). Even during the trial of Jesus, the two enemies, Herod and Pilate, were made friends together, but it was a false peace because it was not based on righteousness. "There is no peace, saith my God, to the wicked" (Isaiah 57:21).

If peace is the possession of adequate resources, then the building of character—our greatest resource—must be paramount in our lives. This is the work of the Holy Spirit of God: "But the fruit of the Spirit is love, joy, peace..." (Galatians 5:22). The Spirit wants to transform us to make us more like Jesus Christ; for as we become more like him, the fruit of the Spirit is produced in our lives. We are prone to want to change circumstances; the Lord wants to change character. We think that peace comes from the outside in, when in reality it comes from the inside out. Character carries with it its own war or peace, depending on who is in control, Christ or self.

Jesus Christ brings peace because he is peace. And the more we become like him, the more we experience peace and share peace.

Peace with God and Man. Being "The Prince of Peace" involves not only his character, but also his cross. "...and, having made peace through the blood of his cross, by him to reconcile all things unto himself; by him, I say, whether they be things in earth, or things in heaven. And you, that were sometime alienated and enemies in your mind by wicked works, yet now hath he reconciled in the body of his flesh through death, to present you holy and unblameable and unreproveable in his sight" (Colossians 1:20-22).

A world falling apart at the seams does not need a definition of that word "reconcile." It represents the deepest longings of the human heart: "Bring us together again!" Human history started with everything in harmony, and then sin entered and separated man from God. Before long, man was separated from man as Cain killed Abel. Sin, the great divider and destroyer, moved through the human race until the earth was "filled with violence" (Genesis 6:11). God judged the world and wiped it clean, starting afresh with Noah and his family. But the poison was too deep in man's system, "for the imagination of man's heart is evil from his youth"

(Genesis 8:21). It was not enough to purge the tree of the bad fruit; something had to be done about the rotten root.

It took God's Son, coming to earth, to strike the final deathblow at sin. At Bethlehem, he was made flesh and entered the human race. At Calvary, he was made sin and bore the iniquity of the human race in his own body. The cross is the great meeting place: "Mercy and truth are met together; righteousness and peace have kissed each other" (Psalm 85:10). It took the blood of his cross to make peace between sinners and God, and one result of this peace with God is peace with one another. Once you have settled the war on the inside, you can settle the wars on the outside. "For he is our peace," writes Paul in a classic passage (Ephesians 2:14). In Jesus Christ, man is reconciled with God and man is reconciled with man.

You can trace this ministry of reconciliation in the Book of Acts. In Chapter 8, the Ethiopian treasurer is converted, a son of Ham. In Chapter 9, it is Saul of Tarsus, a son of Shem. And in Chapter 10, it is Cornelius and his household, sons of Japheth. All of them become members of the family of God! The walls are broken down! "There is neither Jew nor Greek, there is neither bond nor free, there is neither male nor female; for ye are all one in Christ Jesus" (Galatians 3:28). It is not by accident that the cross is a plus sign, for it is God's place of reconciliation, God's place of peace.

Peace in His Companionship. Another factor in Christ's ministry as "The Prince of Peace" is his companionship. His presence brings peace.

As you read the Gospel records, you cannot help but notice that the twelve disciples were often disturbed. You hear them asking, "Who is the greatest?", "What are we going to get?" Unlike their Master, they had unrest and war in their hearts. They found a man outside their group who was casting out demons, and they tried to stop him! When a village refused hospitality to Jesus, the disciples wanted to burn it up with fire from heaven! Instead of being peacemakers, so often they were troublemakers. But before we judge them, we had better look at ourselves. How many times has our presence declared war?

The peace of his companionship is seen especially during those hours just before his arrest and crucifixion. To put it mildly, the disciples were unnerved. To begin with, he had told them that he was leaving them to return to the Father. Then he informed them that one of their number was a traitor. When Peter tried to salvage the situation by affirming his loyalty and courage, a statement that must have heartened the other men, Jesus calmly informed Peter that he, too, would fail by denying the Lord three times! Everything the disciples had trusted was suddenly taken from them. No wonder Jesus said, "Let not your heart be troubled!" (John 14:1).

It was the companionship of the Master that helped to give peace. "Peace I leave with you," he told them, "my peace I give unto you: not as the world giveth, give I unto you. Let not your heart be troubled, neither let it be afraid" (John 14:27). You can go to a drugstore and buy tranquilizers, and perhaps go to a vacation spot and buy rest; *but you cannot buy peace.* Peace is a gift; peace is a Person who is a gift. His companionship brings peace. After those chaotic hours that followed his death, the disciples again met their Lord, and he said to them, "Peace be unto you!" (John 20:19). Then he showed them his hands and his side, because that gift of peace was purchased at the awful price of his own life. For the Christian, peace is not a shallow emotion based on feelings or circumstances. Peace for the believer is a deep confidence and joy based on the victorious work of Christ on the cross. It took his wounds to bring peace to a wounded world.

The fact that Jesus Christ rose from the dead and returned to the Father makes it possible for us to enjoy his companionship today. Today he is our High Priest, our Melchisedec—"King of righteousness ... King of peace" (Hebrews 7:1-3). At the cross, righteousness and peace kissed each other; and on the throne, righteousness

and peace reign through Jesus Christ.
When he is your companion in life, you
experience his peace. "Yea, though I
walk through the valley of the shadow of
death, I will fear no evil: for thou art with
me" (Psalm 23:4). "Fear thou not; for I
am with thee: be not dismayed; for I am
thy God" (Isaiah 41:10).

He gives us his peace through his Word.
"These things I have spoken unto you,
that in me ye might have peace. In the
world ye shall have tribulation; but be of
good cheer; I have overcome the world"
(John 16:33). The companionship of
Christ is not something that we try to
manufacture; it is something that we
accept through the Word of God. He still
speaks through his Word, and as he
speaks, we find his peace filling our
hearts. "I will hear what God the Lord
will speak: for he will speak peace unto
his people...." (Psalm 85:8).

We must remember that God does not
give us his peace so that we may sit back
and enjoy it. He gives us his peace that
we might be able to plunge ourselves
into the tangled problems of a needy
world and share Christ with those who
are at war. This is what Paul termed
his ministry of reconciliation (see
2 Corinthians 5:14-21). When The Prince of
Peace reigns in our lives, then the peace
of God rules in our hearts (Colossians
3:15); and this makes us peacemakers in
the ministry of reconciliation. Because he
is with us, we are not afraid. When Paul
was going through a rough time in

Corinth, the Lord came to him and said,
"Be not afraid, but speak, and hold not thy
peace: for I am with thee" (Acts 18:9,
10). When Paul was arrested in
Jerusalem and it looked like his ministry
was over, the Lord came to him and said,
"Be of good cheer, Paul: for as thou hast
testified of me in Jerusalem, so must
thou bear witness also at Rome" (Acts
23:11). When Paul came to the end of his
journey, a prisoner in Rome, facing death,
he wrote to young Timothy, "At
my first answer no man stood with me,
but all men forsook me....
Notwithstanding the Lord stood with
me, and strengthened me" (2 Timothy
4:16, 17). Paul found peace in the
companionship of Christ, and so may you
and I.

Companionship must be cultivated.
Our Lord does not want to be a divine
lifeguard who is summoned only in
emergencies. He wants to be involved in
every aspect of our lives. He walked
with Enoch and Abraham, and he wants
to walk with us. He talked with Moses and
David, and he wants to talk with us. He
went into the fiery furnace with the
three Hebrew children, and he wants to
share our trials with us. "For ye are the
temple of the living God; as God hath
said, I will dwell in them, and walk in
them; and I will be their God, and they
shall be my people. Wherefore come out
from among them, and be ye separate,
saith the Lord, and touch not the
unclean thing; and I will receive you,

and will be a Father unto you, and ye shall be my sons and daughters, saith the Lord Almighty" (2 Corinthians 6:16-18).

Separation unto Christ does not mean isolation from the real world or insulation from the needs of people around us. Rather, it means single-hearted devotion to him. It means that all we are and have belongs to him, for him to use as he sees fit. Paul expressed it, "For to me to live is Christ" (Philippians 1:21). And Peter said, "But sanctify Christ as Lord in your hearts...." (1 Peter 3:15, *New American Standard Bible*).

Peace on Earth. Our Lord will complete his ministry as "The Prince of Peace" at his second coming. He could have brought "peace on earth" as was announced at his birth, but his people said, "We will not have this man to reign over us" (Luke 19:14). The announcement of "peace on earth" was a valid one; God did not fail—men did. "Suppose ye that I am come to give peace on earth?" Jesus asked. "I tell you, Nay; but rather division" (Luke 12:51). He wept over Jerusalem because they were ignorant of the things that made for their peace (Luke 19:41, 42). There was no peace on earth, nor could there be without him who is "The Prince of Peace." No wonder the Palm Sunday crowd shouted, "Blessed be the King that cometh in the name of the Lord: peace in heaven, and glory in the highest" (Luke 19:38).

The only place you will find peace on

earth today is wherever there is a little bit of heaven. There is peace in heaven, peace purchased by the blood of his cross. There is peace in the hearts of his people who have come to that cross and experienced his salvation. But there will be no peace on earth until he returns and establishes his kingdom. "Of the increase of his government and peace there shall be no end, upon the throne of David, and upon his kingdom, to order it, and to establish it with judgment and with justice from henceforth even for ever. The zeal of the Lord of hosts will perform this" (Isaiah 9:7).

It is then that the great promises of peace found in the prophets will all be fulfilled. The lion will lie down with the lamb. The nations will beat their swords into plowshares. Men will study war no more.

Meanwhile, we wait for his coming. And as we wait, we enjoy his peace and we share his peace with a troubled world around us. We love him; we labor for him; we look for him. We long for that day when he shall reign, and when the breathtaking promises of Psalm 72 will be fulfilled: "The mountains shall bring peace to the people, and the little hills, by righteousness.... He shall come down like rain upon the mown grass: as showers that water the earth. In his days shall the righteous flourish; and abundance of peace so long as the moon endureth." (verses 3, 6, 7).

Even so, come quickly, Lord Jesus!

SEVEN
What Is Your Name?

We have discovered what his name is. The next question is, "What is your name?"

God asked that question of Jacob as he wrestled with him that midnight hour. "And Jacob was left alone; and there wrestled a man with him until the breaking of the day.... And he [the Lord] said unto him, What is thy name? And he said, Jacob" (Genesis 32:24, 27). The name "Jacob" means "supplanter" and carries with it the idea of scheming and lying to get what you want. The first step toward appropriating all that Christ has for you is admitting to him what you really are. What is your name?

Is it Liar, Fighter, Rebel, Pretender, Fearful, Hateful?

What is your name? Admit it to the Lord right now, and let him agree with you. You gain nothing by pretending. Then ask him to forgive you for what

you are, and tell him to make you what
you ought to be in Christ. *Claim for
yourself by faith all that Christ is and all
that he does.*

You see, all of us assume roles in
order to get out of life what we think we
ought to have. Life is dull, so we assume
the role of spectator or entertainer in
order to get some enjoyment. What we
really need is Jesus Christ; for his name
is Wonderful—and that takes care of the
dullness of life.

Life is complicated, and we have to
make decisions; so we assume some role
in order to try to make some sense out of
life. What we really need is Jesus Christ;
for his name is Counsellor—and that
takes care of the decisions of life.

Life is demanding. Some people
assume the role of a tyrant in order to
succeed in this demanding world;
others give up and become slaves or
tools or even invalids. But what we need
is Jesus Christ; for his name is The
mighty God, and that takes care of the
demands of life.

Life becomes narrow and limited. We
feel like we are packed in a coffin.
Perhaps we rebel and try to enlarge our
sphere of experience. Perhaps we give
up the battle and crawl about in our tiny
world, creeping like ants when we
should be flying like eagles. What we
need is Jesus Christ, for his name is The
everlasting Father—The Father of
Eternity—and this takes care of the
dimensions of life.

Life is full of disturbances. Without are fightings, within are fears. There is no peace. A dozen open doors beckon us to some kind of peace—escape, entertainment, alcohol, sex, dope, hard work—and we run from one door to another hoping to find peace. What we need is Jesus Christ; for his name is Prince of Peace, and that takes care of the disturbances of life. "Thou wilt keep him in perfect peace, whose mind is stayed on thee, because he trusteth in thee" (Isaiah 26:3).

What is your name? Jacob admitted his name—and shame—to the Lord; and the Lord changed his name! God said to Jacob, "Thy name shall be called no more Jacob, but Israel: for as a prince thou hast power with God and with men, and hast prevailed" (Genesis 32:28).

God can change your name. "Thou art Simon," said Jesus to Andrew's brother. "Thou shalt be called Cephas," which means "a stone" (John 1:42).

Tell God what you are. Believe what he is. Yield yourself to him.

Put the government of your life upon his shoulder.

When you do, you will discover who he is—Wonderful, Counsellor, The mighty God, The everlasting Father, The Prince of Peace.

And what he is, you will share!

Is the government of your life upon his shoulder?